DINOSAUR WORLD

Relatives of Dinosaurs

Robin Birch

MACMILLAN
LIBRARY

First published in 2002 by
MACMILLAN EDUCATION AUSTRALIA PTY LTD
627 Chapel Street, South Yarra 3141

Associated companies and representatives throughout the world.

National Library of Australia
Cataloguing-in-Publication Data

Birch, Robin.
    Relatives of dinosaurs.

    Includes index.
    ISBN 0 7329 6780 5.

    Dinosaurs – Juvenile literature.
    1. I. Title. (Series: Macmillan young library. Dinosaur world.)

567.9

Edited by Angelique Campbell-Muir
Illustrations by Nina Sanadze
Page layout by Nina Sanadze
Printed in China

Acknowledgements
The author and the publisher are grateful to the following for permission to reproduce copyright material:

Auscape/Jan Aldenhoven, p. 24; Jean-Paul Ferrero, p. 29; Australian Picture Library/© Joe McDonald/Corbis, p. 17; © Jonathan Blair/ Corbis, p. 25; Corbis Digital Stock, p. 21; Kronosaurus, Museum of Comparative Zoology, Harvard Museum of Natural History; photo by Frank Siteman, © President and Fellows of Harvard College, p. 13; Photodisc, pp. 7 (top & bottom), 28; Silkstone Images, p. 6.

While every care has been taken to trace and acknowledge copyright the publisher tenders their apologies for any accidental infringement where copyright has proved untraceable. Where the attempt has been unsuccessful, the publisher welcomes information that would redress the situation.

Contents

Dinosaurs

Dinosaurs lived a long time ago. Some dinosaurs ate animals and others ate plants.

Some dinosaurs were big and some were small.

Reptiles

Reptiles are animals that breathe air, lay eggs and have **scales** all over their skins. Dinosaurs were reptiles.

Lizards and snakes are reptiles.

Dinosaurs were reptiles that walked on the land. They held their legs underneath their bodies, not out to the side like lizards do. There were no swimming or flying dinosaurs.

dinosaur

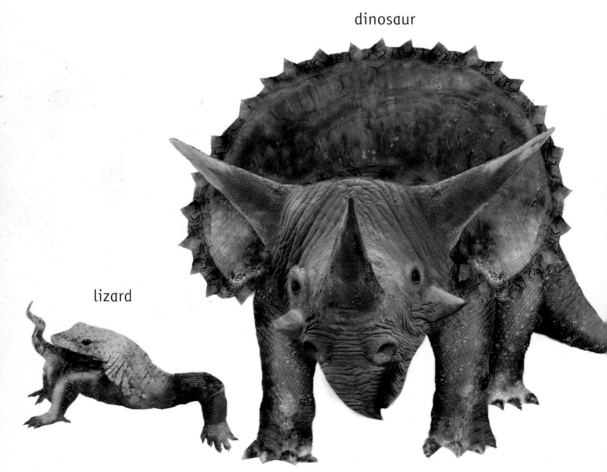

lizard

8

There were many swimming, flying and walking
reptiles that were not dinosaurs, but lived at
the same time as the dinosaurs. They were
relatives of dinosaurs.

Pliosaurs

(say: **plee**-o-saws)

Pliosaurs were very big, swimming reptiles. They lived in seas, lakes and rivers. They ate animals such as other reptiles, fish and **shellfish**.

They had long heads, and their mouths were filled with long, sharp teeth. Their necks were short. They were very fierce and could catch any animals living in the water.

Pliosaurs had a tail and four big, strong flippers. The flippers paddled up and down. Pliosaurs could swim very fast to catch their **prey**.

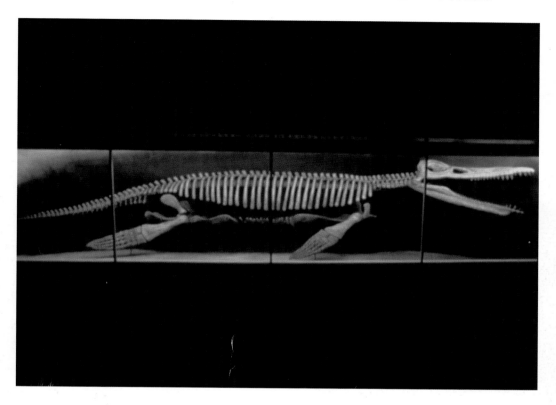

We know what pliosaurs looked like because their bones have been dug up from the ground. These bones are called **fossils**.

Plesiosaurs

(say: **ples**-ee-o-saws)

Plesiosaurs were swimming reptiles that ate fish. They had small heads and sharp teeth. Their necks were long and they could bend them easily.

Plesiosaurs had wide bodies, like turtles without shells. They had four flippers and a tail.

Plesiosurs lived in seas, lakes and rivers. Like other swimming reptiles, plesiosaurs needed to come up to the air to breathe.

Plesiosaurs would have come onto land to lay eggs, the same way turtles do today.

Pterosaurs

(say: **tair**-o-saws)

Pterosaurs were reptiles that flew in the air.
There were many different kinds of pterosaurs.

Pteranodon (say: te-**ran**-o-don) was one of the biggest pterosaurs. It had no teeth. It probably used its beak to scoop up fish from the sea.

The small pterosaur Rhamphorhynchus (say: **ram**-fo-**rin**-cus) had teeth that pointed outward, so it could spear fish in the sea. It had a leaf shape on the end of its tail, to keep it steady when it flew. Including its tail, Rhamphorhynchus was about 1 metre long.

Many kinds of pterosaurs flew over the sea and ate fish. They would have dived into the sea to catch fish like sea-birds do today.

A giant crocodile

There were many types of crocodiles that lived at the same time as the dinosaurs. They were very much like the crocodiles that live today.

One type was called Deinosuchus (say: **die**-no-**soo**-cus). It was a giant crocodile, 15 metres long. It lived in **swamps** and ate fish and small reptiles.

Deinosuchus probably laid its eggs in nests, like crocodiles do today.

Crocodiles today carry their babies in their mouths. Deinosuchus probably did the same thing to carry its babies.

A giant turtle

Several kinds of turtles lived at the same time as the dinosaurs. One of them was a giant turtle called Archelon (say: **ark**-el-on).

Archelon lived in the sea. It was 4 metres long. It had four flippers that paddled up and down, and a short tail.

Archelon had a beak that curved down at the front. It probably ate **jellyfish**, like large turtles do today.

Archelon babies would have hatched out of
their eggs and run together down to the sea,
the same way that baby turtles do today.

Names and their meanings

'Dinosaur' means 'terrible lizard'.

'Pliosaur' means 'bigger lizard'.

'Plesiosaur' means 'near lizard'; plesiosaurs were given this name because they were related to the dinosaurs.

'Pterosaur' means 'winged lizard'.

'Pteranodon' means 'winged, **toothless**'.

'Rhamphorhynchus' means 'beak nose'.

'Deinosuchus' means 'terrible crocodile'.

'Archelon' means '**ancient** turtle'.

Glossary

ancient	from a very long time ago
fossils	things that have been left behind by living things, and have turned into rock
jellyfish	a type of sea animal that looks like jelly
prey	animals killed by other animals for food
scales	small, hard, flat objects on the skin
shellfish	animals that live inside shells in water
swamps	places with wet ground, lakes and streams
toothless	has no teeth

Index